DRAWING SCHOOL

Volume 1

Illustrated by Nila Aye

This library edition published in 2018 by Walter Foster Jr.,
an imprint of The Quarto Group
6 Orchard Road, Suite 100
Lake Forest, CA 92630

Illustrations © Nila Aye

Distributed in the United States and Canada by
Lerner Publisher Services
241 First Avenue North
Minneapolis, MN 55401 U.S.A.
www.lernerbooks.com

First Library Edition

Library of Congress Cataloging-in-Publication Data

Names: Aye, Nila, illustrator.
Title: Drawing school / illustrated by Nila Aye.
Description: First library edition. | Lake Forest, CA : Published by Walter
  Foster Jr., an imprint of an imprint of The Quarto Group, 2018. Contents:
  Volume 1. At the beach -- Under the sea -- On the farm -- At school --
  Volume 2. Around the world -- At the zoo -- Around town -- Let's celebrate
  -- Volume 3. In the garden -- In a fairy tale -- In the past -- At the
  circus -- Beyond our world -- Volume 4. Around the house -- Pets -- At the
  show -- Sports stuff. | Audience: Age 6. | Audience: K to Grade 3.
Identifiers: LCCN 2018005392| ISBN 9781942875659 (vol. 1 : hardcover) | ISBN
  9781942875666 (vol. 2 : hardcover) | ISBN 9781942875673 (vol. 3:
  hardcover) | ISBN 9781942875680 (vol. 4: hardcover)
Subjects: LCSH: Drawing--Technique--Juvenile literature.
Classification: LCC NC655 .D74 2018 | DDC 741.2--dc23
LC record available at https://lccn.loc.gov/2018005392

Printed in USA
9 8 7 6 5 4 3 2 1

MIX
Paper from
responsible sources
FSC® C008080

Table of Contents

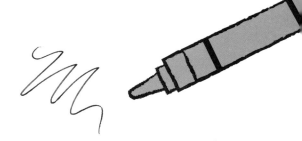

Welcome to Drawing School!

Get your pencils sharpened, your erasers ready, and your artist's hat on—it's time to draw!

Tools & Materials

Pencils
Whether you like a regular pencil or a fancy mechanical one, it doesn't really matter. Just remember to sketch lightly at first, so it's easier to erase. You can always darken your lines later!

Eraser

Eraser
It's a good idea to have a quality eraser on hand, not just the one on the end of your pencil! Just in case you draw any lines you want to change.

Ruler

When you need to make super straight lines, a small ruler works like a charm.

Paper

You can doodle on anything you'd like: a notebook, copy paper, scratch paper...whatever strikes your fancy! But if you're making a drawing you want to keep around for awhile, use some heavier, nicer drawing paper you can get at any arts and crafts store.

Color

Colored pencils, markers, crayons, paints—they're all great! Choose what works best for you.

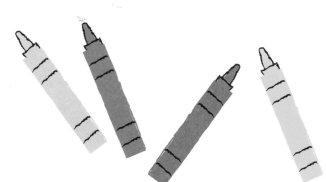

Seeing Shapes

The easiest way to learn how to draw is to look for the shapes and lines that make up what you're trying to draw.

Some shapes are easy to see:

And some take a little more thought:

These are some shapes you should get to know, so you can recognize them easily when you're drawing!

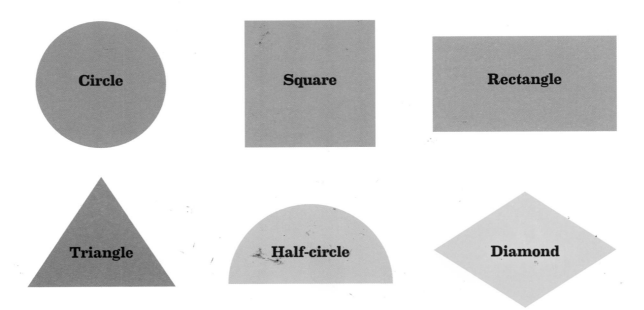

Circle

Square

Rectangle

Triangle

Half-circle

Diamond

Sometimes you'll see other shapes too, like these:

jelly bean shape

"M" shape

What shapes do you see?

Learning Lines

The lines we draw are just as important as the shapes we use.

Lines can be curvy and wavy...

Or straight and angled!

Here are some lines for you to practice:

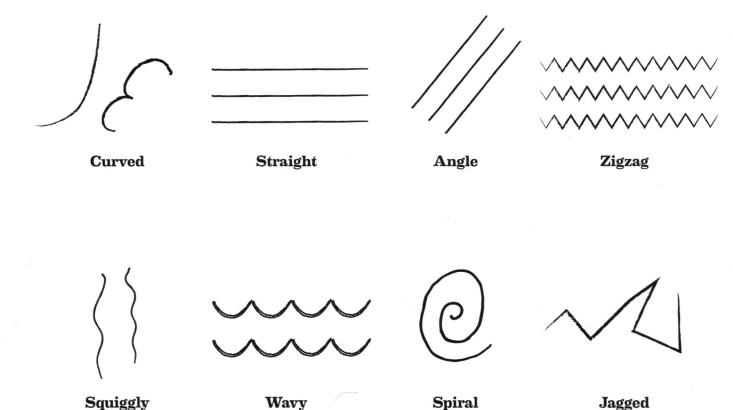

Curved   **Straight**   **Angle**   **Zigzag**

Squiggly   **Wavy**   **Spiral**   **Jagged**

Sometimes it's easier to start a drawing with
an outline of the shape you're trying to draw, like this:

What lines do you see?

At the Beach

sailboat

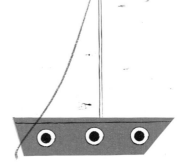

Use straight lines to draw the shape of the boat, and add circles for the portholes.

beach umbrella

Begin with a half-circle, and add two curved lines for the stripes.

Sunny days are here again at the beach! Sailboats and bikinis, palm trees and sand castles—they're all here on the sandy shores. Get your shades ready. Let's draw a day at the beach!

Add a mast and triangles for the sails. Ahoy, mate!

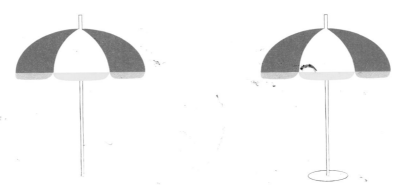

Fill in the colors and add the stand. Now you've got some cool shade!

sun

This friendly sun begins with a big yellow circle.
Add two circles for the eyes and curved lines to finish the eyes and smile.

waves

To show movement in water, like waves, just add some "wavy" lines!
Start with a "U" shape, and then connect it to two or three others.

palm tree

Start with a spidery shape, using long, curved lines for the palm leaves.

Now add triangles for the rays of the sun, and color it all in. Shine on!

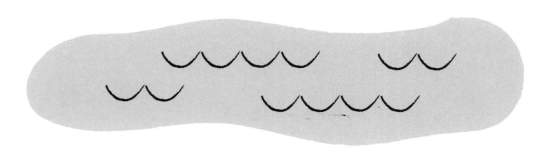

Vary the length and number of waves you make, so it looks like a real ocean shore.

Draw a long, thin trunk, and then add the details on the trunk.

beach ball

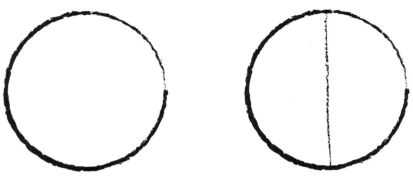

Begin with a large circle, and draw a straight line right down the middle.

bikini

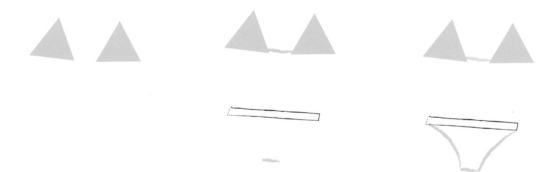

Draw two triangles for the top, then add a thin rectangle and curved lines for the bottom.

sunglasses

These cool shades are really just two half-circles with some straight lines.

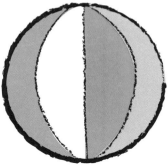

Then draw two curved lines, one on each side. Use bright colors on your beach ball!

Add some squiggly lines for the ties, and then draw some stripes on your suit!

Color your shades, and add some bling if you want!

sand castle

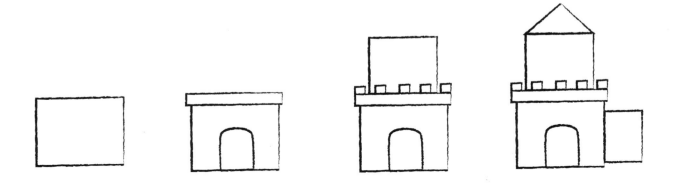

Build this sand castle with rectangles. Start with a base, and add the door and tiny squares on top.

pail

For the pail, start with an oval at the top, then draw a curved line for the bottom and connect it with straight lines.

16

Then add the rest of the castle, using more rectangles and triangles for the tops.

shovel

For the shovel, begin with a half-circle, and then draw the handle around it.
Draw two upside-down "U" shapes for the bottom.

round seashell

This shell is like a big half-circle with a little triangle at the bottom.

spiral seashell

Start with a circle, then draw a rounded triangle shape on the right side.

anchor

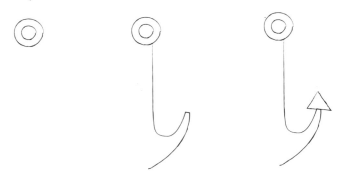

Begin with a small circle within a circle. Then use curved lines to draw one side of the anchor, and add a triangle tip.

Add a rectangle to fill out the bottom, and then draw the details.

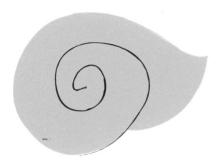

Now add the spiral in the center of the shell.

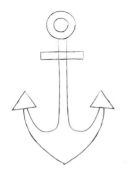

Now fill in the other side, and add a rectangle near the top and rope around the anchor.

lighthouse

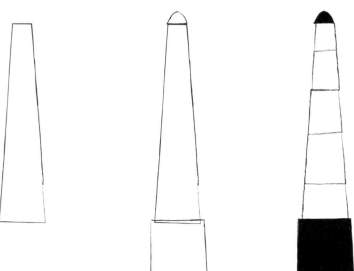

The lighthouse is wider at the bottom than it is at the top,
so your straight lines need to point slightly toward each other.

sailor

Let's start with the sailor's hat! Once you have that in place, add his face and shirt.

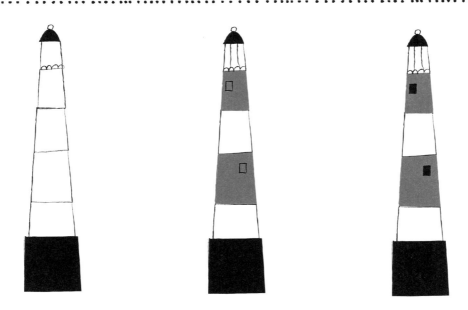

Add a square base, a triangle top, and some bright stripes to your lighthouse.

Then draw his wide-legged pants and give him some shoes too. Ready to set sail?

cruise ship

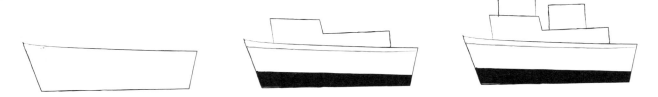

Draw a rectangle that is a little taller on one side. Then add the shapes for the rest.

tourist

Start with a circle for the head and add a half-circle for his hat.
Then draw his face and add his colorful shirt.

camera

  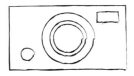

Draw a rectangle first, then add the details with smaller circles and rectangles.

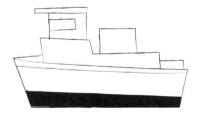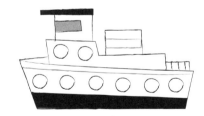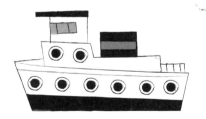

Add stripes, circles for the windows, and all the other details!

He needs bright shorts, and socks with sandals, of course! Don't forget to add his fanny pack.

Add the final details, and this camera is ready to capture your day at the beach!

Under the Sea

yellow fish ....

Start with a yellow triangle for the body. Add its fins, mouth, and tail next.

pink tropical fish ....

This colorful fish's body is a circle with a triangle at the end.

The ocean is filled with cool creatures that are very different from what we see on land! Explore it by drawing different sea animals, like tropical fish, mighty whales, puffy puffer fish, and friendly dolphins. You might even find some sunken treasure!

Now add the rest of the details: the eye, green fins, and stripes.

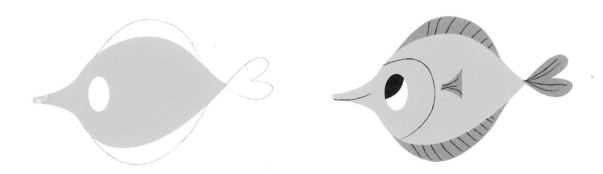

Draw curved lines for the fins, and add a heart-shaped tail. Then finish off the details!

scuba diver

Use ovals for the face and mask, and curvy pointed lines for the hair. Then add the curved body.

coral

Coral looks like a willowy underwater tree. Start by lightly sketching the base, then add curved lines for the branches.

seaweed

Waving in the water, seaweed is all curvy lines!
Start with one line in the middle, and build out from there.

The fins are just two curvy triangles. Add a rectangle for the oxygen tank too!

Fill in with color, and add some tiny dots for details.

Once the lines are in place, add tiny straight lines to show all the leaves.

jellyfish

This friendly fellow starts with a smiley face inside an oval!

dolphin

Begin with a rounded triangle shape for the body.
Then add curvy triangles for the fin, flipper, and tail, and an oval for the eye.

Add some curvy lines for the rest of his body, and some long, curved lines for his tentacles.

Use two small round shapes for the mouth and a tiny circle
for the blowhole on top of her head!

sea lion

For this sweet sea lion, draw an oval shape for the head first.
Then add the long, tapering body and two flowy triangle shapes for the back flippers.

crab

This funny crab is all circles and skinny legs! Start with his body and eyes.

shark

Start with two curved lines for the body, like a crescent moon shape.
Then add his eye and fin, and the bottom half of his body.

Of the two front flippers, the one that's closest to you should look a little bigger.
Give her some whiskers too!

Then draw his legs. Don't forget the claws!

Use triangles for his other fin and tail, then draw in his gills and teeth.
He looks too happy to bite!

lobster

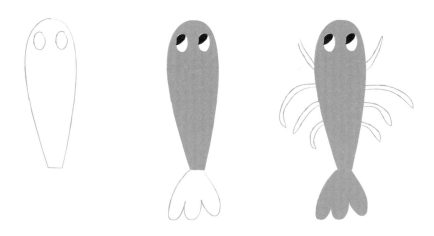

Give this lobster six legs and two big front claws.

octopus

Begin with a rounded rectangle for the body.
Then draw her face, and add four of her curvy tentacles.

Use long, curved lines for its antennae, and some smaller detail lines to show the sections of the shell.

Add four more tentacles, and then draw little semi-circle suckers on each of her tentacles.

sea turtle

The turtle's shell is an oval with a pointed end, and his head is a small oval.

whale

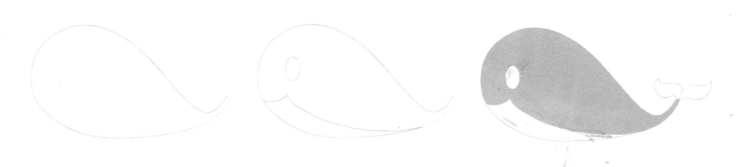

This whale's body looks like a giant raindrop on its side, doesn't it?

treasure chest

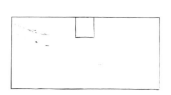 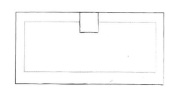 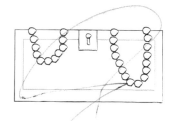 

Draw a rectangle first, and add a smaller rectangle inside and a square for the lock.
Draw small circles for the pearls and trim too.

Add curvy triangle shapes for his flippers, and then draw the pattern on his shell and body.

Use curved lines for her tail, her belly, and the spout of water at the top too!

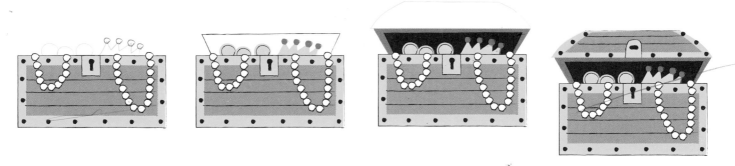

Then add the lid and more treasure inside. Happy treasure hunting!

seahorse

Begin with a circle for the head and add a long, skinny mouth.
Draw curved lines for the body and a spiral for the tail.

sea urchin

One oval plus two circles will start your sea urchin!

Fill it all in, and add a triangle fin. Draw a spiky spine down the back,
and then give her some stripes—and eyelashes!

Then add some spikes of all different sizes to show off its prickly powers.

sea star

Start this simple star with the first two sides of a triangle.
Then add four more of the same!

stingray

Two curved lines make a giant smiley shape. Add a curved line
for the head and draw the rest of the body.

puffer fish

Draw a big circle to start, then add a face and a triangle fin.

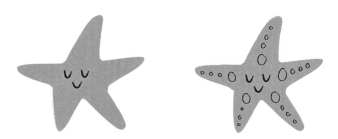

Tiny circles show off this super starfish's suckers.

Use curvy lines for the tail, and add all the final details too.

Use round lines for the face, but short, small triangle shapes for the puffer's spikes.

On the Farm

cow

Start with a small rectangle for the head and a bigger one for the body. Then add the face and horns.

horse

Draw a triangle for the head with a circle at the end.
Then add triangle ears and rectangles for the neck and body.

Mooooo. Oink. Baaaah. There's so much to draw on the farm! You can draw a crowing rooster, a rumbling tractor, and a big red barn. The sun is shining, the pigs are rolling in the mud, and the cat's asleep in the hay. Let's get drawing on the farm!

Add the udder, legs, and tail. Color her in, and don't forget to leave room for some spots!

Finish off by drawing the legs, mane, and tail. Giddyup!

goat

This hairy goat starts with a simple oval for his head and a circle for his eye.
Then add his ears and horns.

sheep

Start with a squiggly cloud shape. Then add a "U" shape for the sheep's face.

Add a few angled lines for his body.
Use short, curved lines to show his furry belly, and little "U" shapes for his feet.

Draw another big fluffy cloud shape for her body, and draw her legs and tail too.

duck

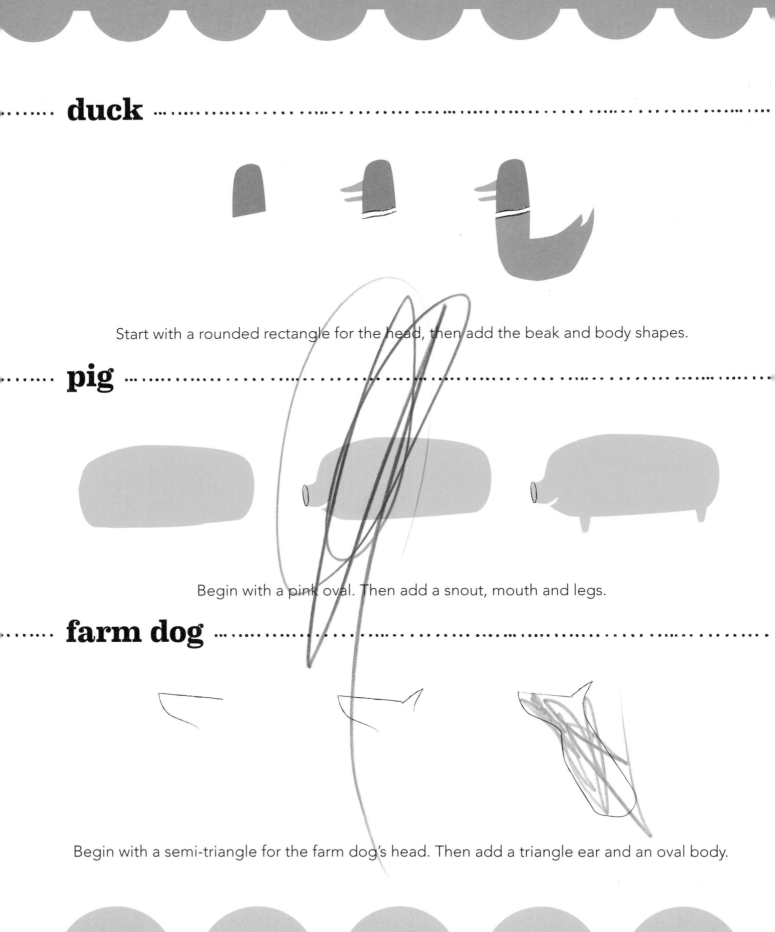

Start with a rounded rectangle for the head, then add the beak and body shapes.

pig

Begin with a pink oval. Then add a snout, mouth and legs.

farm dog

Begin with a semi-triangle for the farm dog's head. Then add a triangle ear and an oval body.

Then add the feet, eye and wing.

Add the ear and the other two legs. Finish up with an eye, another ear, and a cute curly tail.

Add his legs and tail, and his friendly face. Awww, it looks like he wants a treat!

hen

Start with an oval shape for the head, and use a half-circle shape for the body and tail.

chick

The chick's body is an oval with a little tiny triangle at the end. Add a circle for the eye.

rooster

Draw a circle for the head, then make a ruffled bottom and add the eye.
Use curved lines for the body and feathers.

Add the feet, beak, and comb and wattle (the red parts). Use a "U" shape for the eye.

Two tiny triangles make the beak, and three lines make each leg.

Add the legs, beak, and comb and wattle. Cock-a-doodle-doo!

scarecrow

Use a half-circle for the hat, and another for the face. Add rectangles for the body and arms.

corn

Use a long skinny, oval to start, then use curved and angled lines for the leaves.

crow

Start with a rounded shape for the crow's body, and use curved lines for the wing.

More rectangles for the legs, and the patches on the shirt too!

Draw a grid of slightly curved lines to show all the kernels.

Fill it in with black, and add feet and a yellow beak!

farmer

Begin with a flat oval and a curvy line for the hat. Then add his face and rectangles for his body.

tractor

Start with circles for the wheels, then add the other parts of the tractor one shape at a time.

bale of hay

Draw two rectangles, and add zigzag lines on the left and right sides.

Draw his arms and boots, and don't forget his pitchfork and pail!

Add the tread on the tires and the steering wheel, and color the tractor a bright red.

Use more zigzags to show the texture of the hay, and add straight lines for the binding.

sunflower

Draw a brown circle for the center, then fill in around it with yellow oval petals.

farm cat

Start with ovals for the head and body, and triangle ears.

mouse

Use curved lines for the outline of the body, and draw big ears and tiny feet.

Add another color of petal behind the yellow ones, and then draw a green stem and leaves.

Use curved lines for the cat's tail, and add little triangles for stripes.

Add a nose, whiskers, and tail, and maybe even a tiny piece of cheese!

barn

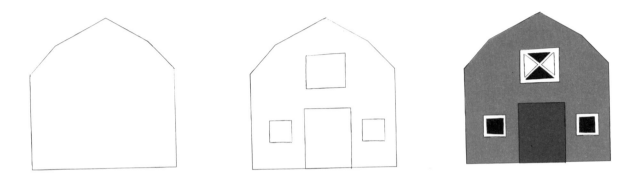

Start with a simple rectangle. Then add a triangle roof and squares for the windows.

farmhouse

The roof looks like a slanted rectangle.
Once you have the roof, add straight lines to draw the rest of the house.

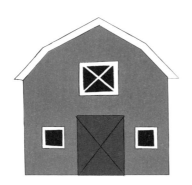  

Add all the details, including the weather vane on top, and then paint your barn bright red!

Add the windows, doors, and chimneys, and you've got a farmhouse!

At School

school bus

We're drawing this bus from the wheels up! Start with two circles and a big yellow rectangle.

backpack

Start with a rectangle for the front, then add on the rest of your pack using curved lines.

Today's lesson: your classroom! Jump to the head of the class by learning how to draw everything you see at school, from the yellow school bus and the books you carry to your backpack and even your teacher too. Class, let's begin!

Build your bus from there, adding the top and the windows and details. Everyone on board!

Add the straps, zippers, pockets, and all the rest!

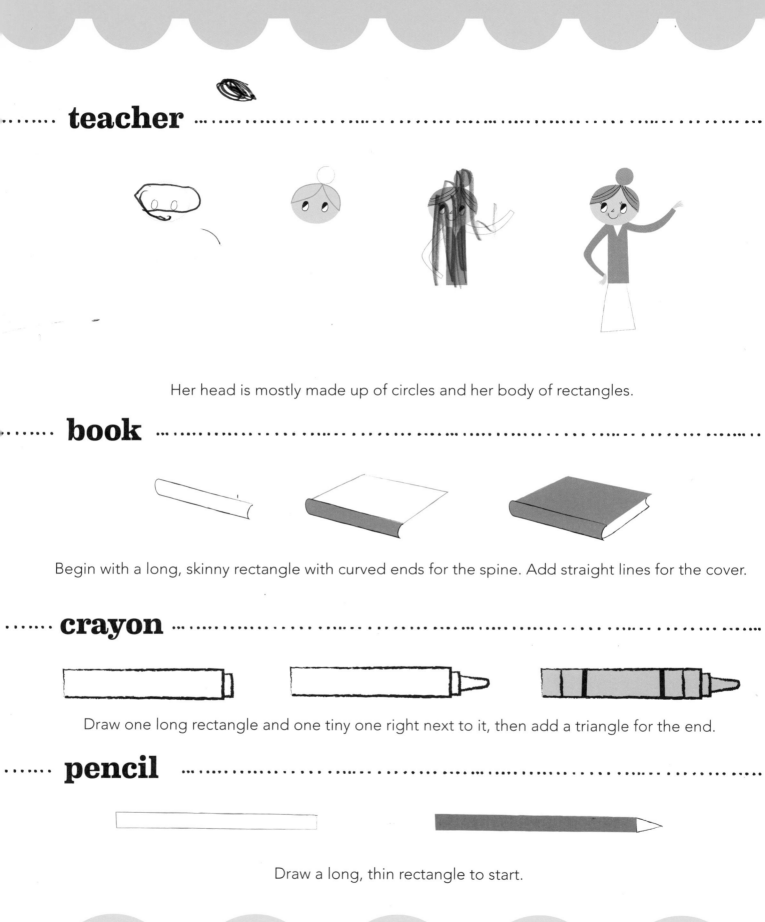

teacher

Her head is mostly made up of circles and her body of rectangles.

book

Begin with a long, skinny rectangle with curved ends for the spine. Add straight lines for the cover.

crayon

Draw one long rectangle and one tiny one right next to it, then add a triangle for the end.

pencil

Draw a long, thin rectangle to start.

Draw her arms, legs, and face, and then color her in. You get an A+!

Create a back cover and draw in some pages.

ruler

Use another skinny rectangle for the ruler, and add little lines for the marks.

Then add a triangle for the tip.

desk

For the top of the desk, use a slanted rectangle. Then add rectangles for the sides.

chair

For a simple chair, draw two rectangles for the back and seat. Connect them with four straight lines.

globe

Draw a circle to start. Add the pattern. Hey, those are the continents!

Now draw the legs and add the rest of the details.

Add four legs and the edge of the seat. This chair is brown, but yours can be any color!

Then draw the stand and add color.

schoolhouse

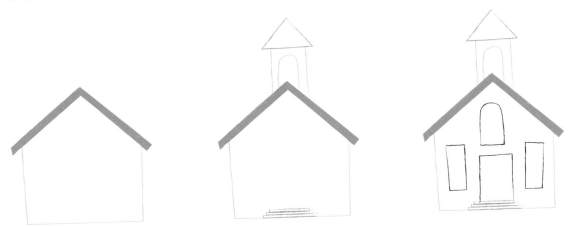

The schoolhouse is like a square with a triangle on top. Draw the bell tower too.

swing set

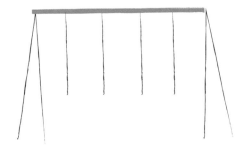

Draw a long, thin bar at the top, and use straight lines for the legs and swings.

slide

Draw two long, curved lines to start the slide. Use two more curved lines to draw the back side.

Then draw the doors, windows, and the school bell at the very top. Time for school!

Then draw the seats of the swings, and use bright colors to fill them in.

Next use angled lines to draw the ladder, and straight lines for the steps.

Check out the other volumes in this series!

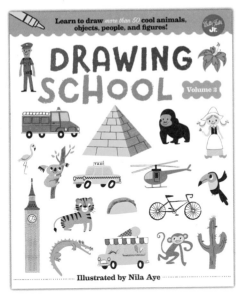

9781942875666

9781942875673

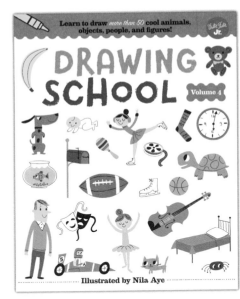

9781942875680

About Nila Aye

After graduating from her sell-out show at Central Saint Martins in 1995, Nila became a firm favorite of the London illustration scene. Nila is influenced by mid-century design and children's books from this era. She describes her work as "Retro modern with a cute twist, and a touch of humor." Nila's style is loved by adults and children alike and is popular with fans around the world.